Leadership

How To Communicate Efficiently In Order To Influence People And Generate In-depth Conversation With Anyone And Everyone

(A Step By Step Guide That Will Teach You How To Improve Your Social Skills And Take Control Of Your Emotions)

DariuszSchantl

TABLE OF CONTENT

The Existence Of Sacred Connections 1

Displaying A Humble Attitude 6

Relationships And Interactions Between Leaders And Their Teams 12

The Crucial Role That Trust Plays In Communication 21

Is It Predestined For Someone To Become A Leader, Or Does It Depend On Their Qualities? 33

Governance; Leadership Is Taking Responsibility For Doing The Right Things 39

Respect Together With Maturity And Objectivity 57

Having A Mentality That Is Open To Learning 66

Accuracy, Adaptability, Educational Capability, And Operationalization 76

You Can Only Get Things Done If You Delegate. 83

- The Leader Who Is Able To Communicate 94

Be Aware Of What Is Happening In Your Environment 98

The Struggles In Private 108
Leadership Is A Way Of Behaving Rather Than A Title Or Position. 121
Learn Your Own Method Of Leadership. 130

The Existence Of Sacred Connections

The interest in a group is supported by a multitude of spiritual conventions. Worship and other gatherings, such as going to chapel or participating in a prayer gathering, have the potential to be sources of social assistance. These activities also have the potential to provide a sense of having a place, security, and belonging. It has been shown that strong connections can build wellbeing and strengthen future, which may be why one study discovered a strong relationship between chapel participation and improved wellbeing, mind-set, and wellbeing.

Some people are able to overcome traumatic experiences like kidnapping, war, and detainment by seeking solace in a profound sense of being or religion. Real-life examples of this interconnectedness through spirituality depict this process. There are a lot of instances in which spiritual people find ways to get past the test and continue on with their intentional living; when this happens, they take a step back and keep going.

If you have a strong spiritual perspective, it may be easier for you to find meaning in the challenging situations that life throws at you. In one piece of research, there was a woman who overcame post-traumatic anxiety following an abduction and assault by coming to terms with the fact that her traumatic experience served as a stage for her self-improvement, compelling her to evaluate her life and find ways to improve it on an ongoing basis. She attributes her capacity to move forward with her life and her commitment to a profound spirituality to the fact that she has these things.

The spiritual exercise of recognizing the interconnectedness of all life is one way to help cradle the pain that comes along with difficult experiences. According to the findings of a number of studies, if we are able to kindly assist ourselves in times of disappointment by remembering that disappointment is a part of the shared human experience, then that particular instance transforms into one of fellowship rather than confinement. When our stressful and distressing experiences are framed within the context of the fact that countless others have endured similar adversities, the blow isn't as difficult to take when compared to how difficult it would have been otherwise.

The observance of a specific religious practice may bring about an indirect improvement in one's health. This is on account of the fact that numerous religious practices include guidelines for treating one's body with kindness and avoiding engaging in practices that are detrimental to one's health. Research demonstrates that individuals who practice a religion or a confidence convention are less likely to smoke or abuse alcohol, commit crimes, or get involved in violence. On the other hand, these individuals are more likely to participate in precautionary behaviors such as wearing seatbelts and taking vitamins. Perhaps this is because of the precepts that are taught in these religions and confidence conventions.

People who have a strong spiritual life have a significantly lower risk of passing away, according to the findings of a comprehensive study that compared a profound sense of being and religiousness with various other factors that influence one's health. According to the primary author of the study, the life-extending benefits of most spiritual sense of being could be compared to eating a large quantity of fruits or taking blood pressure medications. This comparison was made using calculations. Even though there are some researchers who believe that the extent to which most religious and spiritual practices are beneficial to health is exaggerated, the vast majority of researchers agree that there is a positive correlation between religious and spiritual practices and improved health outcomes.

Displaying A Humble Attitude

It takes a powerful person to act with humility, and it takes an even more powerful leader to recognize their own limitations. Respect between a leader and their followers is built on the leader's demonstrated ability to act with humility. It should be considered the cornerstone of successful leadership.

Recognizing your own shortcomings is essential to developing humility. It is not necessary to carry out this activity in front of a group of people. However, you must be able to look at yourself truthfully in the mirror and acknowledge the areas in which you could improve. As you shift your focus from being me-driven to being team-driven, humility helps you become a better individual and, as a result, a better human in society.

There is no correlation between humility and either weakness or permissiveness. It is neither overestimating nor underestimating the value of an individual. The trait of humility is not synonymous with low self-esteem or actions that are counterproductive to one's goals. In conclusion, it is not a path that leads to one's own degeneration.

To be a humble leader requires nothing more than the simple act of being humble. It means letting go of your pride and putting the requirements of other people ahead of your own. It means choosing the morally superior path and carrying out one's actions with the larger good in mind rather than one's own personal gain. It is a setting in which effective leadership can take place.

If you do not have strong leadership, you will eventually find that you have no one left to lead. In the beginning of their careers, many managers have the mentality of "I'm the boss, so do as I say." This strategy is utilized by the majority of clinical leaders, which is completely understandable. Because of your background as clinical professionals, you were trained in this manner. You will quickly find out that adopting an autocratic leadership style will have a negative effect on both your ability to lead effectively and to exert influence as a leader.

Certain leaders exhibit a lack of humility by being indifferent to the needs of their team members, indifferent to the feelings of team members, irritable, and easily angered. These leaders are known to make snap decisions, speak with a sharp tongue, and act in a hasty manner. It is an indication of poor leadership and has its roots in pride. These leaders will be responsible for commanding the support of the team. Nonetheless, it is done out of fear. The leaders of the team will never receive the full respect of their teammates, and the team will not follow them beyond the scope of their current authority.

Your ability to empathize with other members of your team and understand their needs and emotional positions can be strengthened by humility. Additionally, it is the capacity to forgive oneself as well as one's teammates in the event of unfavorable circumstances or results.

Serving others effectively requires one of its key components to be humility. Humility and shifting the focus to the team are hallmarks of servant leadership. The leader is made humble by the responsibility to serve the cause or by the opportunity to lead. It is making connections with people in order to direct them on their journey.

There is a chance to improve one's management skills from every manager. You will pick up ineffective management strategies from a poor manager, and you will also be able to feel the erosion of respect that the manager experiences. Take into consideration the fact that these leadership strategies are ineffective in leading the team. You will learn what strategies actually work if you work under a competent manager. You will gain an understanding of the various ways in which an individual's skills can be utilized in a manner that is beneficial to the organization.

Building the sincere trust of one's teammates is among the most significant advantages that can come from practicing humility. The ability to trust others is brittle and should be treated with the utmost respect. In the following chapter, we will discuss the strategies that can be used to earn the trust of the team even if you do not currently hold an authoritative position.

Relationships And Interactions Between Leaders And Their Teams

The effectiveness of a team is directly correlated to the leadership of that team. They have the extraordinary opportunity to invigorate the workings of the organization with which they are affiliated. They also have a significant bearing on how the individuals with whom they collaborate interpret the various circumstances in which they will find themselves.

A process that needs to be carried out with the utmost care is the selection of individuals who will be put in a leadership role in the organization. It is essential for leaders to be adequately prepared for the roles they will play because they will be responsible for determining the pace of work, the nature of the working environment, and the performance of the employees they will be managing.

The mindset of a leader, in addition to other necessary skills such as managing one's time effectively and making sound decisions, will have an impact on the group of people with whom they will be collaborating. The following are some examples of how leaders can influence the dynamics of the teams that they are responsible for.

Strong leaders are able to instill a sense of dedication and responsibility in their teams.

The workplace is fraught with a significant number of sources of stress. The combination of lengthy working hours, a large number of deliverables, and impending due dates is enough to convince almost anyone to give up. Leaders have the ability to assist their teams in working through challenging circumstances. They assist those around them in better managing the tasks they have at hand so that they can perform their jobs in a more calm and collected manner.

Leaders can work with their teams to develop strategies for more effectively managing their time, allowing them to complete a greater number of tasks within the allotted amount of time. They are able to empathize with the challenges that other members of their team are facing, and as a result, they are able to offer the necessary support.

People who work for effective leaders find that they are more motivated to complete the tasks they have been assigned. They value the fact that their leaders are able to understand them, and as a result, this appreciation serves to reinforce their determination to complete the work.

Effective leaders are able to produce results.

The leaders of the team are the most intelligent members. They are aware of the steps that need to be taken on their end in order for their teams to achieve the desired outcomes. They execute their plans effectively in order to meet the deadlines. They come up with a goal that is attainable and communicate it to their teams in order to establish clear standards.

When you are strategizing, you should also try to anticipate potential roadblocks and ensure that there are backup plans in place. Although leaders tend to have a positive outlook, they also make it a point to plan for the worst-case scenario so that their teams are always prepared.

In addition, those in leadership roles are responsible for ensuring that they have access to all of the relevant data in order to be in a position to make important judgment calls on which their teams can rely. Their teams have faith in the decisions because they exude confidence without coming across as arrogant. The members of the team are aware that their leaders are the most qualified individuals to make the difficult decisions.

Because their teams are unified behind them, leaders are able to deliver positive results to their organizations. They have a reputation for being trustworthy, credible, and the most qualified members of their teams to steer them toward victory.

What are some of the benefits of reading this book?

This book explores the idea of servant leadership from a completely fresh perspective, focusing on the behaviors of

Christians both as individuals and in the roles they play within organizations. It addresses the following aspects in an effort to provide guidelines for implementing servant leadership in one's personal life as well as in organizations, including but not limited to the following:

Conviction: It analyzes the development of God's Leadership Sketch as it unfolds throughout the Bible, thereby laying a solid groundwork for the conviction that is required to be a Servant Leader.

Confession: This book examines the history of the Church and draws attention to the errors that our ancestors committed by disobeying the Not-So-With-You command that was given to them by our Savior Jesus Christ. Because of this, it is considered Confessional by the readers.

Behaviours That Can Be Observed This book provides a set of seven behaviors that we call the DEEP BHC Behaviours. Based on my research, these are the behaviors that are characteristic of a servant leader. The readers will be able to observe servant leadership as a result of this.

Self-Development: In this step, we will map the DEEP BHC Behaviours to ten characteristics that will assist us in establishing those behaviors as habits. All of these characteristics and behaviors have illustrations and stories from the Bible to back them up. This helps the readers work on their own personal development.

Personal: The addendum includes information about a 360-degree survey that was conducted on the behaviors of the DEEP BHC and was based on my doctoral thesis. This brings the topic of servant leadership closer to home for the reader.

The addendum includes a Practice Guide so that the leader can put into action the actions that they determine are necessary based on the results of the 360-degree assessment. The reader will find this aspect of Servant Leadership to be very practical.

Beneficial: The addendum contains a template that can be used to record significant changes that one can observe in themselves, as well as the impact those changes have on their life and work as a result of reading and acting on the advice in the book. Because of this, it is helpful to the person reading it.

This book is being used as the basis for an educational program that is currently being developed and implemented. Participation from the readers is encouraged so that the journey may proceed. Because of this, Servant Leadership Development is now possible. Presented with assistance for the reader.

Enduring: A Coaching support system is offered to readers in order to assist them in transforming their "good intentions" into concrete actions. The reader will find this to be Enduring as a result.

The Crucial Role That Trust Plays In Communication

A person who believes they are valued will almost always go above and beyond what is expected of them.

Because of this, it is essential that everyone be capable of acting independently rather than merely obeying the orders given to them by their manager. It is a good idea for the company to have the ability to do its own thing, which is why this is a good idea.

You need to reach the point where employees are so dedicated to their manager that they would do anything for them. When something like this occurs, it indicates that the team is functioning effectively and that the manager is doing an excellent job in terms of both the results and the relationships.

If you want to get as close to this ideal scenario as you possibly can, the first thing you should do is make it a policy to always take responsibility for your employees' mistakes and to defend them in any situation in which it is necessary without ever sending them to the gallows.

This straightforward idea, which is covered in every management class, is the most challenging component for a manager to put into practice because it can sometimes result in an unsatisfactory performance, and other times it can result in an earful or even a more serious threat. The entirety of this for actions that are not carried out by us and for which we do not feel responsible.

Because of this, there are some people who are not really prepared to take on such a responsibility because it requires a great deal of maturity.

On the other hand, even if we are convinced that our worker is solely to blame for the incident, we are unable to absolve ourselves of the responsibilities that are attendant upon our position.

There are a few possible explanations for why one of our workers would make a mistake, including the following:

1) He has not received the appropriate education or training; 2) No effort was made to help him comprehend the significance of that particular activity; 3) He has been given a task that is beyond the scope of his capabilities; and 4) His work was not checked for accuracy before it was finished.

In each of these situations, we are the ones who should really be held responsible because we are the only ones responsible. It is far too simple to place blame on our workers, sometimes even in their absence, without providing them with the opportunity to discuss the factors that led to their decisions.

The majority of the time, it concludes with someone saying something along the lines of "I told Titius to do it, but he must have forgotten," followed by a response from our boss that says "We know Titius is a...".

We come out unscathed and have the impression that the problem has been solved, but the reality is that we lost a significant chance to earn the respect of our staff members.

In the unfortunate event that this discharge of responsibility should absurdly take place in front of them, the relationship between us will unavoidably be compromised, and we will never again have their trust.

A self-respecting manager will immediately understand when we are taking responsibility for what has happened in defense of our employees, and they can only appreciate this attitude if we do so. This is something else that needs to be taken into consideration, and it is important.

1. They have value as people in and of themselves.

If you believe that life has value, then you must also acknowledge that people, and specifically all people, do have value.

What should be done about violent criminals whose only goal in life is to injure and kill innocent people? Do they not have a right to live?

Sure.

But before we do, let's ponder this. When someone's actions are so despicable that they put others' lives in danger, the death penalty is a justifiable form of punishment. However, you will find that this is the very last option available to you in our judicial system. Why? Because people in general place a high value on life. We want to believe that there are opportunities for do-overs. We believe in giving other people the benefit of the doubt and the chance to put things right.

And if you were wrongfully accused of murder but found guilty anyway, would you want to be sentenced to death as quickly as possible?

It's possible that she has some habits that are incredibly annoying, like filing her nails during meetings. It's possible that when she talks, her voice can be heard all the way across the building.

However, if she possesses a brain, she possesses the potential to have insightful ideas. If she has friends, then it shows that she is succeeding in some aspect of her life.

And if she was hired, it's because someone, possibly even you, believed she was capable of doing the job.

Therefore, treat her with the dignity that is due to a fellow human being.

2. The point of view of each individual is important.

There will be times when you and the other members of your team will disagree.

That's not a problem.

It's not always the case that you're right.

It is healthy to engage in debate on various issues. For instance, even if you and another person are engaged in the same activity, you may be able to gain something useful from the experiences of the other person. Wouldn't it be interesting to know what her secret is for success if she's had more of it?

Everyone has thoughts and ideas. Because we are all unique individuals, it is to everyone's advantage to learn from one another in order to progress. If you enjoy playing basketball, do you think that shooting hoops by yourself will help you become the best player you can be?

No, you can't prove how good you are without the help of other people.

Your fellow employees can help you improve your mental agility.

Then you should follow suit for them.

Make it a routine to take an interest in the lives of those around you.

People enjoy focusing the conversation on themselves. You should not restrict your inquisitiveness to the people you are responsible for leading. Make it a practice to be interested in the things that are going on in the lives of other people instead. This will give you the opportunity to gain an understanding of how the lives of other people are distinct from your own. You will gain access to a wide variety of sources of motivation as a result of this, which you can then utilize in your leadership roles.

You might want to think of some questions to ask new people when you meet them. Pay close attention to what they have to say and show that you are engaged in the conversation while they are speaking. You can demonstrate this by fixing your gaze directly on the person who is speaking to you and waiting for them to finish before offering any of your own thoughts or opinions. Avoid trying to outdo other people.

When you're having a conversation with someone, make it a habit to keep asking questions rather than offering suggestions or advice. When it comes to gaining knowledge, nothing beats talking to other people about their own life experiences.

You can forge a profound connection with other people by making an active effort to learn about the details of their lives. The vast majority of people will love you once they realize that you appreciate them in both their personal and professional lives. Because the vast majority of people take pleasure in chatting about themselves, they will find it easy to engage in conversation with you and will consider you to be approachable.

Pick and choose the individuals with whom you engage in social interactions.

You will not have enough time to learn about all of your followers if you are in a leadership position. Choose a small group of people to connect with rather than trying to socialize with all of your followers at once. You are free to refer to this collection of individuals as your "mastermind group." This group ought to be made up of adherents who are knowledgeable and capable enough to have work assigned to them.

By organizing a mastermind group, you can concentrate your efforts on cultivating meaningful relationships with a smaller pool of individuals. You should entrust the more significant responsibilities to this team. This strategy works wonderfully for introverted business leaders. When they have to deal with a large number of people, introverted leaders feel exhausted.

Is It Predestined For Someone To Become A Leader, Or Does It Depend On Their Qualities?

Let's investigate whether a person's birth into a leadership role is predetermined by fate or the result of the attributes they demonstrate throughout their lives.

Do you have faith in the concept of 'fate'? Whether you believe it or not, the essential question is whether or not it is possible for it to be predetermined in advance (by destiny) that a man will be categorised as a leader. Is there an all-seeing, all-powerful being who looks down from up high and says, "Yes! You are going to be the leader of the whole world!"?

The reality is that it can never be written in advance; rather, in order to reach the quality of a leader, one will have to make use of one's own qualities and seize the opportunity to become one. How could you possibly join their ranks? Let's talk about this some more.

If he seizes the opportunity at the correct time to become a forerunner, a regular guy has the potential to rise to the position of leader. It is not always required for him to do something that makes him look like a leader, as it may actually make him look like a fool if he does it. You need to have the following attributes within you to generate excitement in the people who are around you in order to become a leader. Let's get a better understanding of how it is feasible for a regular man to rise to the position of a leader.

Exhibit Your Capabilities When They Are Needed:

It is usually suggested to just demonstrate your talent when it is required of you. If there is no reason for you to do so, displaying your expertise is not required. You need to maintain your composure and look around to see if there is a way for an everyday man like you to show off your abilities. If you do discover one, you should always make an effort to provide it the greatest performance possible. Under these conditions, you need to step up and assume the role of leader in order to provide assistance to the other members of your group until the mission is finished. You will subsequently be referred to be a "leader," which is the genuine transition from a common guy to which you will have undergone. You can be seen as a leader by simply seizing the opportunity and utilising your skills at the appropriate time. In this way, you can elevate yourself from the position of a common man to that of a figure of authority.

If, on the other hand, you try to show off your skills without their being any demand, you will be considered as a fool with an arrogant temperament, and you will never be labelled a leader.

Keep Your Eyes on the Prize:

A common man typically engages in more talk and less action than a leader does, which is one of the key differences between the two. Additionally, they think less and work more, see less and do more, but a leader does the reverse of these things. It follows that in order to earn the title of "leader" as opposed to "common man," you must act in a manner consistent with that of a leader. Additionally, it will increase the likelihood of you becoming a leader in the future.

You have to come to terms with the fact that you are not capable of finding answers to all of life's questions. Instead, in the words of Albert Einstein, 'think more.' This is due to the fact that if your imagination has a good enough quality to think more and more, you will be able to solve a lot of difficulties in your head. You can find solutions to a greater number of problems in a shorter amount of time than you could have in the real world. You need to cultivate your imagination in order to be able to think more and more, which is what is required of a leader, rather than a simple common guy, in order to solve the problem psychologically. Therefore, if you are working harder to rise from the ranks of common men to those of leaders, you will need to look further than what you are now doing. There are going to be a lot of individuals who do what you're doing, and there might also be a lot of other people here with the same fearless mindset. The difference won't appear unless there are variations in people's imaginative capacities. To put it another way, this is the point at which a leader diverges from an ordinary guy.

Governance; Leadership Is Taking Responsibility For Doing The Right Things

Taking up responsibilities and being accountable for your actions is a sign of good stewardship. The responsibility of the leader is to ensure that the members of the team are held accountable by setting an example and removing any obstacles in the way. Accepting the results of an endeavour, whether they are positive or negative, is an essential part of being accountable.

As servant-leaders, we have an obligation to accept responsibility not only for our own acts but also for those of the team as a whole. You are more important to your team than they are to you. As leaders, we receive compensation based on the success or failure of our team's performance. If the team is unsuccessful, then so are we. To ensure the success of the team, it is our responsibility as leaders to eliminate any obstacles that may arise. The accomplishments of the team will serve as our yardstick. Think about the difficulties that are being caused by the obstacles that the team is facing. Determine ways to overcome the challenges and remove them from the equation. So, how exactly do we put stewardship into practise? It all starts with setting an example for others to follow.

Taking the Lead Through Example

In order to provide a good example for others, we need to take responsibility for our own behaviour. It is incumbent upon us to serve as a model for others to emulate. Then it is incumbent upon us to adhere to the same guidelines, policies, and regulations that we have imposed upon the team. For instance, the manager cannot simultaneously like a post on social media and provide performance feedback to a member of the team for engaging in the same behaviour. Additionally, in the event that a stringent travel provision is put into effect, the leader is not permitted to remain at the most opulent hotel in the city or to commence stringent expenditure and buy a luxury vehicle. Who are some of the most prominent leaders in the world today? What emotions does it evoke within you? Are you getting any worse? Are you irate? Feeling frustrated? If you are hurt by what was said, look at yourself in the mirror, think about what you've been doing, and try to improve.

What do you think? When you don't lead by example, everyone on your team has the same impression.

Consider your options before you take any action. Each of our acts has the potential to have an effect on our team. Always keep in mind that the audience and your team are watching you perform. The higher your rank, the more space you have to work with. The mentality of "do as I say, but not as I do" is detrimental to the morale of the team, and it also undermines your credibility as the leader of the group. This double standard upheld by the leader undermines the morale of the group and has the potential to be disastrous. The team will not sense the empathy and respect that you are attempting to convey to them if you continue in this manner. Imagine that each member of your team has their own individual bank account. Every act of trustworthiness, attentiveness, and relationship-building, among other things, constitutes a modest deposit into an account. Over the course of time, you build a strong partnership with your staff and a nice nest egg for yourselves. Every time you don't set a good example for others to follow, there will be money taken out of the account. The acts of the leader will decide the total amount that will be withheld from the account. Large withdrawals will be made until there is nothing left in the account as a result of treachery, whether actual or perceived.

As a direct consequence of this, you no longer have the authority to supervise the team. The ability to lead is certainly a luxury. To be given the responsibility of leading a group in which they have placed their trust is a tremendous honour. This is a privilege that should not be taken for granted. We have a responsibility to protect that faith by always acting in the way that is in the team's best interest and by serving as a model for others to follow. By setting an example for our team and beginning to practise what we preach, we are able to show them what is possible and begin to live up to the standards we have set. Because the leader is also participating in our activities, our teams begin to believe that it is feasible for us to reach our goals. One of the keys to encouraging members of your team to follow you is to set a good example for them to follow. It is a relatively insignificant act, yet it will result in significant returns and deposits into the group's online savings account. With enough time, the squad will eventually follow you wherever you go.

You may easily apply the concept of leading by example to your leadership in a number of different ways, including the following:

Always put yourself in others' shoes and be willing to go the extra mile.

Maintain the same level of adherence to the guidelines that you would anticipate from the rest of your team.

Take care not to interrupt any other members of the team, especially if you have something negative to say about someone else's habit of doing so.

If you let the team have an early start on the day, you should do the same thing yourself. If you stay and finish the work, the other members of the team will feel guilty.

Take a minute to reflect on your approach to leadership, as well as your principles and the choices you make. Think about whether or not there are any changes that need to be made.

Compassionate feeling

To put it another way, empathy is the capacity to put oneself in the position of another. When you have empathy with a certain circumstance, you are able to put yourself in that scenario and picture how you might react. Because it enables you to offer assistance to individuals in your immediate environment, possessing this ability is emotionally significant.

When people you care about come to you for guidance, you will be able to take into account their past experiences and empathise with what they are going through because you will have experienced similar things. People are brought together by empathy, which fosters connections between individuals even when there aren't many words said. Empathy should absolutely be one of the top priorities that you focus on developing as part of your social skill set.

There are a few distinct varieties of empathy to take into consideration. Others are sparked by something that the other person says or does, while others originate from feelings that are more natural to you and have always been there. It is quite interesting to take a closer look at the factors that make this comprehension possible. You can actually discover a lot of new things about yourself by doing so. The following are some of the most typical manifestations of empathy that you will encounter in your life:

Affective: [key] This variety of empathy is based on the concept that you are able to comprehend another person to the extent that you can identify with the feelings that they are experiencing. For instance, if your friend is going through a breakup and starts crying because she misses her ex-partner, you would probably be able to relate to and empathise with the feeling that she is experiencing because you have been there yourself. When you have this level of comprehension, you are able to approach the scenario from a point of worry or care since you know what they are going through.

You must avoid being overly emotionally invested in the predicament of the other person. This is a trap that you must avoid falling into. Because of how easily you can relate to the situation, you run the risk of eventually developing sentiments of personal discomfort as a result of this. When we go through things in life, it becomes simpler for us to emotionally relate with other people who are going through the same things that we have gone through because we have gone through them ourselves. To guarantee that you are helping the other person without inadvertently causing harm to yourself in the process, you will need to strike a delicate balance.

Cognitive empathy is distinguished from emotional empathy by the fact that it is experienced purely in the mind. It is the ability to allow yourself to think the way that this person is thinking without placing yourself into the emotional state of being that the other person is in. Although it is still a sort of empathy, cognitive empathy is more detached than affective empathy since it requires you to maintain a position of objectivity towards the circumstance.

Your ability to empathise with others can be improved by practising with this as a starting point. A skill is something to be proud of when the person who possesses it can listen to someone else describe an issue and yet come up with a few solutions depending on the way that the other person is thinking. You won't be as vulnerable to harm because you won't be emotionally invested in the situation. When you are attempting to show cognitive empathy, you should be careful not to come across as uncaring. If you don't show any sign of friendliness in either your tone of voice or your demeanour, people will misinterpret the behaviour you exhibit.

Because it involves the body, somatic empathy is distinct from other types of empathy. This occurs when you are able to identify with another person on such a profound level that your body responds with some form of physical manifestation. This might manifest itself as a dull aching in the stomach, for instance. If you have ever been exposed to unfavourable information, you have probably had a sick feeling at the very bottom of your stomach. This is a response that occurs in the body. It is not always necessary to have a negative reaction to something. There is also a physical sensation associated with happiness. Empathy can take many forms, but one of the most powerful and beneficial is known as somatic empathy.

If you give yourself permission to experience an excessive amount of negativity all at once, this particular type has the potential to become the most annoying of the three. Even if the circumstances that are causing you to feel sad, afraid, or embarrassed are not directly related to you, those emotions nevertheless have the capacity to bring you down. Know that there is nothing wrong with you or with the way that you work; when you can experience these feelings physically, all that is happening is that you are simply in tune with the empathic aspect of your personality.

No matter how many of these sensations you've had or how few, there is always room for improvement in your abilities. When you can demonstrate empathy for another person, you will develop into a more attentive listener. Active listening is a quality that should always be a goal of yours, regardless of the kind of the discussion you are having or the company you are keeping. When combined with empathy, this becomes a lot easier to do since you will be able to listen and establish your own ideas a lot more rapidly. Empathy allows you to put yourself in the shoes of another person. Your suggestions will be full of helpful advise because they will be based on the information that has been provided to you as well as your judgement of what should be done.

NOT SUFFICIENTLY GOOD

The fundamental problem is a fundamental sense of insecurity on the part of the individual. Children who have difficulty regulating their emotions in social situations, such as when they shift from thinking "no one wants me around" to "I'm going to be the boss," are said to be navigating an internal security disorder. Whether it be due to genetics, a product of their nature, only-child syndrome, or just their personality, these younger children merely require some additional support in order to increase their sense of self-worth.

For instance, Angela does not believe that she is deserving, which is why she hops from group to group, unsure of how to integrate herself into the life of another person. Because of this, after only one statement, she begins to loudly complain, "Why don't you want to be my friend?"

Angela has interpreted this as a sign that she is not deserving of friendship, despite the fact that no one brought up the subject of friendship; rather, they were only trying to determine where Angela's garden will be built.

John, another kid, has come to the same conclusion as well. He is also attempting to become a part of a group, but the only way he is aware of doing so is by bothering the other children, poking fun at them, mocking them, slapping them on the butt, calling them ridiculous names, and generally being a nuisance to them in the hopes that they would pay attention to him. Because he, too, does not value himself on the inside, he has engaged in a potentially harmful engagement in the hopes of gaining new friends. He is unable to attract love and attention in a healthy way since he is clueless as to how to do it.

Mike is the same in every way. After a few minutes, he begins to hit, punch, grab the ball, and then flee away from the situation. This kind of thing takes place a great number of times. A tendency that I find particularly noteworthy is that these youngsters are not insecure children in and of themselves. They are competent in the activities they undertake at home, in the classroom, and in other settings as well. They have self-assurance in their respective fields. They are proficient in reading, writing, speaking, and presenting oneself to others in a positive manner. When requested, they are able to share valuable life lessons with other children. They do have a tendency to be domineering, but they are still determining their worth in collaborative areas, and this causes them to be a little bit insecure.

Respect Together With Maturity And Objectivity

"The seventh incarnation of Durga is the goddess Kalaratri, whose name literally translates to "one who dispels darkness or puts an end to ignorance." She is shown as the one who vanquishes evil and is the fiercest and most terrible of all the gods. She has a black complexion, untamed hair, four hands, three bulging red eyes, and a tongue, and she rides a donkey. She is also known by the name 'Kali matha.' Kali was conceived with the purpose of slaying the demons Shumbha and Nishumbha, who had already vanquished Lord Indra. Raktabija, an additional demon, is dispatched to do fight with Kali on their behalf. He was blessed with the ability to produce an exact duplicate of himself with each drop of his blood that spilled onto the ground. As soon as Kali was aware of this, he assassinated Raktabija and drank all of his blood, preventing any of it from falling to the ground. After that, she dispatched Shumbha and Nishumbha and reclaimed the realm that the other gods had misplaced. She wields a vajra and a knife in combat against negative energy and bad forces. She removes the cloud of anxiety that hangs over the lives of her followers, empowering them to face the world without trepidation. Those who worship her have access to authority as well as a variety of other leadership skills, according to Grandma.

The temple had a shock in store for me. On that particular day, the adornment of the goddess Durga was quite distinctive. The significance of this avatar was explained to me by my grandmother, thus even though the statue was designed to look menacing and angry, the fact that it did not worry me in the least that it looked so menacing is due to the fact that I understood the meaning of this avatar.

On that particular day, I was given grey clothing as a gift, and I knew that my mother would have the characteristics that are associated with the colour grey. After finishing my meal in a hurry, I went straight to my room to seek for the present for the following day. I walked into the room and saw a small gift package sitting on the bed, along with a handwritten letter that read, "Do you have any grey colour traits? It is time to investigate what lies within you. Take prompt action." When I opened the present, I found an attractive grey crystal with the inscription "Authority, Maturity, and Neutrality" engraved on it.

I went ahead and listened to the voicemail that had been left for me by my mum.

The hue GREY is associated with NEUTRALITY as well as PROTECTION. This grey stone is said to represent the power of transformation, maintains energetic equilibrium, and helps keep individuals grounded in reality. When it comes to their roles, women frequently have to make decisions that are devoid of emotion and bias and behave with maturity. Their position of authority requires them to make decisions in a consistent and impartial manner. The characteristics of the grey colour will assist you in using your authority responsibly and living up to your duties.

ASKING FOR ASSISTANCE

After getting back to our fire station, I gave my wife, Debbie, a call, and I explained everything that took place during the meeting. She was pleased that the fire chief had challenged me and that God was working in my heart to change the cycle of anger that I had been displaying. The following morning, I gave our pastor Ward Smith a call, explained what had happened, and asked for his assistance. Ward mentioned that he had a small booklet for us to use, and that the first meeting of our group will take place the following Sunday after church. When we first met, I had no idea what to anticipate, but I was aware that I required assistance and that I would be held accountable for my actions. Ward gave me a small booklet on Moses titled "His Anger and What It Cost Him." the booklet was very thin and small.22

I had familiarised myself with Moses through numerous readings of the Book of Exodus, in addition to witnessing Charlton Heston represent him in the film The Ten Commandments, which was released in 1956. After someone questioned me about my anger, I was able to see the life of Moses and his struggle with the same issue from a completely new perspective. In addition, I had a deeper comprehension of the negative effects that my anger had on the people in my immediate environment, particularly on my family. I came to realise that a state of simmering rage is both a sign and symptom of discontent, which is related with a deficiency of joy in our life. My research led me to the conclusion that fear and fury are related. Fear that I will not be able to control the future or anything else that happens in life. I also started to become aware that my anger was making people avoid being around me.

In addition, I came to the realisation that leaders who are angry are leaders who are useless.

5. CAPABILITIES IN CONSULTING ••••

Consultants contribute their knowledge to the process of identifying organisational issues, supporting the investigation of those issues, and recommending potential solutions. In this chapter, we will examine your job as a consultant, as well as provide you with some ideas on how to structure open communication, work with feedback, and deal with resistance. A well-known proverb is that "a consultant, in order to be worth their salt, must give honest judgements, and not necessarily those that they think the client would like to hear." This is a good way to explain the work of a consultant. In this chapter, we will discuss the function of the internal and external consultant, as well as their characteristics and talents, typical issues, and potential roadblocks.

When you work in recruitment, you frequently take on the function of consultant. As a result of this, you are provided with some tribal knowledge and have an insight of the cultural nuances and people systems in the organisation, both of which can be taken into consideration while making changes. Your cultural awareness should not be undervalued when it comes to the implementation of solutions that call for transformation. In addition, if you are an internal consultant, you will have the opportunity to observe the long-term advantages of the work that you conduct within the organisation.

Recruiters frequently provide support for change management in their organisations. This support may include the development of specific solutions or even the project management of change projects that are proposed. The focus of these projects is typically on the optimisation of processes, although they are not restricted to that alone; for instance, they may also involve the management of processes. Internal consultants are frequently found to be concentrating on implementation and continual improvement, and the function of a recruiter has traces of this kind of work as well. For instance, it is typically up to them to continue refining an organization's recruiting strategy, and because of their close interaction with customers, they can maintain an interest in monitoring how well the strategy is working after it has been implemented.

When compared to external consulting, which is more process-oriented in its approach due to the milestones that are contractually tied to payment, internal consulting can be more organic and ambiguous in nature. In most cases, an internal recruiter isn't even aware that they are functioning in the capacity of an internal consultant. However, if you find yourself in a position in which you are serving in this capacity, you should make sure that you exhibit the characteristics of an effective consultant.

One "What on Earth Just Happened?"

Will Keiper, our fearless leader

In the beginning of my career as a leader, I proudly repeated something I had previously heard other managers say: "The most important assets in our organisation walk in and out of this building each and every day." Despite the fact that delivering those words made me feel good about myself, as I looked around the room at some of those "assets," I saw polite half-smiles, slowly nodding heads, and perhaps some sidelong glances. My statements did not ring true with them, and neither did they with me.

During that time, I had the mindset that such human "resources" were somewhat interchangeable. To ensure that my actions were in line with my beliefs, I made it a habit to conceal most forms of compassion from them. I was aware that there was a possibility that there would come a time when it would be essential to have a challenging talk about ways in which performance could be improved or possibly termination. I am embarrassed to admit that, due to the fact that I knew far too much about them personally, I purposefully avoided feeling sorry for them. It was about preventing myself from having feelings that I knew could be upsetting.

I also tried to avoid having lunch and dinner with the "troops" whenever it was at all possible. Simply put, this was one more way that I cut myself off from "the most important assets in the organisation." Even though I maintained this detached stance for longer than I like to confess, I eventually came to the realisation that it was not beneficial to the organisation, the people who worked there, or to me. As a result, I embarked on the path of transformation, which I will explain in greater detail in the following paragraphs.

These relics of bygone methods of leadership stand out like a sore thumb in today's world. You only need to glance around to see for yourself how true this statement is. The fact that humans are imperfect but also capable of remarkable change is, of course, something that will never change. These kinds of transitions frequently occur when large sea changes transform the safe zone represented by the status quo into a hazardous zone. Because the currents of today are both more powerful and more changeable, it is abundantly evident that maintaining one's status quo is no longer an option. The time has come to demonstrate compassion for others, which is a necessary component of strong and well-rounded leadership.

Having A Mentality That Is Open To Learning

A. Alter your persona in some way

Few individuals have a true understanding of the power that identity possesses and how adaptable it may be. There are a lot of people who don't change for the better for the most of their lives because they aren't aware that they have the option to fully reinvent who they are. If they did this, they would find out that there is a significant amount of room for improvement in their situation.

I know from personal experience how liberating it can be to make changes to one's identity. My first significant step towards a new identity was making the decision to have my work have an effect on millions of people. I quickly came to the conclusion that the only way for me to achieve this goal was to view myself as a "high-performer." In order for me to accomplish my lofty goals, I had to raise the bar for what I considered acceptable. How did I make this change to who I am?

I just made the decision to carry it out.

I made the decision that beginning at a specific point in time, I would conduct myself as though I were a top performer and would continue to make that decision. After that, I questioned my understanding of what it meant to perform at a high level. What set the best performers apart from the rest?

One of the responses was that high performers follow their promises, both to themselves and to others. This was mentioned as a characteristic of high performers. They gradually gain more self-assurance in their capabilities as they continue to do so consistently, which leads to positive outcomes. As they continue to be successful in reaching their goals, they begin to believe that they are capable of achieving ever more ambitious targets, which they do.

So, I proceeded in that manner. I began with manageable objectives and continued to succeed in accomplishing each one. I established daily routines for myself, and I remained committed to them for several months. As time went on, I improved my performance to a great level.

Another instance of my changing my identity is demonstrated in this example.

For many years, if somebody asked what I did for a living, I'd tell them, "I write books and sell them on Amazon." At some time, I came to the realisation that I needed to make the transition from saying "I write books" to saying "I'm a writer." As a result, I began telling myself, "I'm a writer," and I envisioned how I would present myself to other people. The identity of "I'm a writer" gave way to "I'm a six-figure author" for me at that point. This phrase has come to serve as my daily motto. When I needed to make a decision that had to do with my company, I would always ask myself the following questions: "As an author who makes six figures a year, can I afford to not do this?"

For instance, am I in a financial position where I can forego purchasing a course, comparing pricing, or writing consistently?

How you perceive yourself to be is very important. Your identity will frequently become your reality, particularly when a significant amount of time has passed. You have to think of yourself as an extremely capable student. It is imperative that you have faith in your capacity to learn virtually everything you set your mind to. Your approach to education will undergo a radical change once you acknowledge that you are a very effective learner. You will become incredibly resilient as a result of it. Even with all of its ups and downs, you will be able to enjoy the learning process more as a result of this. And as a consequence of this, it will make it possible for you to acquire more skills and information, which will in turn make it possible for you to accomplish many of your objectives.

In light of this, if you now consider yourself to be a bad learner, you should realise that this perception does not have to be permanent. You have the opportunity to reinvent yourself as a dogged learner who is not willing to give up on their goals today. Imagine for a moment that you had the ability to acquire whatever knowledge that you desired; how would it make you feel? In what ways would it make your life better? What kinds of fun and useful new abilities might you be able to acquire?

Always keep in mind that learning is a process that cannot be avoided; thus, why not make your own learning more effective and efficient?

There are three different kinds of employee-employer relationships in corporations: isolated, closed, and open.

1) Isolated Relationship: If an employee doesn't participate in the corporate's recreational, promotional, or departmental activities in any way, the possible inference drawn is that he or she is only linked with the corporate or organisation over money and is least concerned about the development of the corporate; in other words, he or she

continues to be selfish by being a non-attached member in the corporate. This is known as an isolated relationship. He or she remains uninvolved in the affairs of the corporation regardless of what transpires. These kinds of workers need to be weeded out via analytical investigations, and once identified, they need to be encouraged to change their perspective. On the other hand, workers of this type are more likely to leave their jobs and relocate before a considerable period of time has passed. In order to integrate employees who behave in this manner into the mainstream of the company, appropriate checks and remedies are being sought.

2) CLOSED RELATION: If an employee participates in the corporate's recreational, promotional, or departmental activities on an intermittent basis but never gives suggestions for possible improvements,

the possible inference drawn is that he or she is partially attached to the 'vision and mission' of the corporate or organisation but does not suggest initiatives for the development of the corporate (either at lower level or at higher level). This is the case if the employee does not give suggestions for possible improvements. These are the kinds of workers who should be incorporated into the configuration of the corporate structure by welcoming their participation in various development efforts. This will ensure that these employees never consider leaving their current position in search of a new one elsewhere. In this method, the incomplete link would end up being a complete connect.

3) OPEN RELATION: If an employee participates in the corporate's recreational, promotional, or departmental activities wholeheartedly

without making excuses and always pops in to give suggestions on being welcomed, the inference drawn is that if proper financial and professional care is taken of this type of employee, this type of employee would bring positive change in the corporate, adding value to it. If this type of employee is not welcomed, the inference drawn is that this type of employee will not be welcomed. This kind has absolutely no plans to resign from the corporation in its current manner.

From a psychological point of view, it is recommended that corporate-employee relations be analysed based on "psychological reveals," in which "group psychology concepts" and organisational behaviour are mapped on to construe the employees' subconscious states, which are revealed consciously through corporate participation. It is possible to classify the degree of connection that exists between an organisation and an individual based on the behavioural pattern and professional execution style.

LEARNING OBJECTIVE FOR CORPORATIONS The corporations should pay attention to the type of employee, and as a direct result, watch the impending layoffs, evaluations, and improvements.

Accuracy, Adaptability, Educational Capability, And Operationalization

Acuity is characterised by an increased awareness of oneself, one's actions, one's environment, and the effects one achieves. Developing your acuity and awareness is an extremely valuable talent to have since it will enable you to determine whether or not the actions you are taking are leading to the results you desire. You now have options to examine as a result of assessing the actions you took and the results they produced. Whoever has the most options available to them (as a result of their adaptability) will typically have the most impact in any given circumstance. Once you have taken a look at the results that have already occurred, you may find that you need to make some adjustments and change your direction significantly in order to better define your outcomes.

This may necessitate the acquisition of new knowledge or even just a shift in viewpoint. You are now aware of the results and the changes that need to be made in order to improve them; all that is left is for you to internalise your newly acquired abilities or approaches and apply them in the appropriate manner.

If you wash, rinse, and repeat the procedure described above on a consistent basis, you will not only be able to maintain an up-to-date skill set, but you will also form a habit of engaging in self-improvement and personal development. When you appropriately direct and re-direct your actions based on the analysis of your outcomes, you will discover that your results are of a significantly higher quality and that you are able to accomplish your goals in a significantly shorter amount of time.

The impact of this consistent improvement will propel a team forward via the development of the individual, resulting in members of the team who are secure in their abilities and who have a culture of excellence deeply embedded in them. This is one of the ways that a leader can maintain the long-lasting respect that is necessary in order to manage a team over the long run.

Personal charisma and influence on others

Personal effect can be described as charisma; nevertheless, although charisma is difficult to measure, its power transcends social standing and riches and eliminates preexisting biases. It is thought that charisma is an extremely potent gift that is only bestowed onto a select few, despite the fact that it is a gift of a mysterious nature. In point of fact, charisma is the capacity to leave a remarkable, emotionally charged, and enduring impact on the people we come into contact with. individuals who have charisma and know how to use it effectively are able to naturally influence individuals in their environment because they exude both expertise and confidence.

When it comes down to it, charm and likeability are ideas that are difficult to fully comprehend. But ultimately, what matters is how the people around you experience themselves when they are in your presence. We might concentrate on the characteristics of mysterious communicators and leaders from the past in order to learn from the lessons they have for us. Because of my experience working in the sales profession, I've learned certain effective tactics that help me make a bigger impact in whatever contact I'm a part of. As was discussed before, the first steps consist of developing one's self-awareness and flexibility, which are then followed by education and execution. Working on the individual aspects and leveraging them against one another will greatly enhance your perceived charisma and the personal impact you make on the people you meet. As an example of leveraging, proper posture will greatly improve your speaking voice. The areas you will focus on to achieve your goal of having a greater personal impact will be localised.

Signs that you need to work on improving your charm and personal influence include the following:

My nervousness gets the best of me, especially when I have to do presentations.

I prefer to keep to myself.

The earth is something that I find myself staring at quite frequently.

I frequently get an aggressive attitude.

It's not always easy for me to put into words how I'm feeling.

I've been told that I speak in a mumble.

My posture isn't the finest, and I tend to 'hunch' my back rather frequently.

My thoughts and ideas are frequently dismissed or disregarded.

I have some reservations.

There are instances when I have trouble making decisions.

I always seem to get the response "yeah, but" whenever I talk.

People frequently misunderstand my motivations.

I get nervous when 'opening' new clients or speaking to new people.

I get on well with clients but struggle to 'close'.

I find myself using filler words like "um" and "uh" quite frequently.

You Can Only Get Things Done If You Delegate.

People who have a lot on their plates should learn how to assign tasks if they want to get anything done. The average individual simply does not have enough time in the day to get everything done that needs to be done. People who are productive eventually realise that it is essential to delegate tasks in order to make progress. Productive people are also aware of what tasks can and should be assigned, as well as the most efficient way to carry out those tasks.

What is outsourcing if not assigning to trained professionals activities that we ourselves are unable to complete? Whether it be the design of a website or public relations, the cleaning of our home or the preparation of food for a cocktail party, outsourcing involves delegating these tasks. Delegating tasks appropriately may be beneficial to the profitability of an enterprise as well as to the growth and development of an organisation. When responsibilities are shared occasionally, employees have the opportunity to broaden their skill sets and learn how to contribute more value to the organisation.

When we are short on time and energy, or when we do not have the necessary expertise, it makes sense from the point of view of both time management and quality control to assign a particular project and remove it from our plate so that we can concentrate on things that only we can accomplish. This allows us to work on things that only we can do. If we hoard all of the key responsibilities, it might lead to actual or perceived controlling behaviour, which is counter-productive. If we hoard all of the important obligations. Setting priorities is the first step in learning how to delegate effectively, which is a crucial ability to have.

Not simply the tasks, but also the responsibilities should be delegated. Promote buy-in for the project at hand and loyalty to you by delegating the responsibility for leading a component of the assignment. Rather than merely allocating work to someone, which limits the sense of ownership, you should delegate the obligation. Give that person the opportunity to shine by letting them demonstrate their inventiveness, analytical ability, talent for managing systems and operations, troubleshooting prowess, and whatever else is required to successfully manage that area of the project. You make sure to maintain an eye on the bigger picture while doing everything in your power to ensure that the individual in question has the authority and resources necessary to fulfil his or her responsibilities.

Recognise that the way you do things is not the only way. It's possible that this will lead to some pleasantly unexpected outcomes that turn out even better than you had hoped. It is important to remember that everyone has a distinct perspective on how a task should be handled, and you should trust the individual to whom you've delegated the responsibility even though they may have a different strategy. There is frequently more than one way to arrive at the correct result. Put your attention on accomplishing what you need to do in the allotted amount of time. Never engage in micromanagement.

Provide direction that is unambiguous and ample background knowledge. Describe the overall scope of the project and how the component that has been delegated fits into it. Make sure the person understands the project specifications for what will be delegated to them and provide those specs. Ensure that the individual in question have the authorization to perform what must be done, as well as the money, the staffing, and any other resources that may be required. It is important to have a clear understanding of the project's milestones and its due date. If assistance is required, make sure you are available.

Train yourself to recognise when it is appropriate to delegate a project or components of it by first establishing goals and objectives for your company, backed by strategies and action plans that will assure their realisation. This will teach you when it is appropriate to delegate a project or elements of it. Be open and honest about the timeframe, as well as your strengths and limitations. Focus your attention on the outcome as you outsource or delegate the tasks that you are unable to complete yourself. Create a reliable group of people that are eager to assist you in achieving your objectives.

IN ORDER TO MAKE THE TRANSITION TO LEADERSHIP, TRAINING AND DEVELOPMENT ARE REQUIRED.

It is the responsibility of those in leadership positions to ensure that other leaders are trained to replicate their successes.

According to a quote attributed to William A. Beckham, "the ultimate test of leadership is not whether a person can lead, but whether that person can teach others to lead in the same way."

To those who look to Jesus as the paradigm for discipleship, Jesus not only teaches, but he also lives life with people and encourages them to change their attitudes and behaviours by participating in life with them.

innate as well as learned qualities of leadership

When he was writing about the spiritual gifts and the teaching that explains them, the Apostle Paul mentioned that God chooses which talents each believer will have based on his or her sovereignty.

Paul also urged believers to pursue gifts and taught Timothy and Titus how to become leaders by providing them with training and teaching. Paul was aware of the fact that one's spiritual gifts might be either inherited or acquired.

The teaching of the Apostle Paul includes a list of spiritual gifts. In addition to it, he discusses the process that was used to obtain the donations. According to Romans 12:6 and Ephesians 4:7, each person is given at least one gift that is distributed based on the grace of God. It is at the Holy Spirit's discretion and according to his will that each talent is distributed (1 Corinthians 12:8–11; Ephesians 4:11). Paul acknowledged and preached that God chooses leaders according to his sovereign will. Paul makes it quite clear that God is the one who decides which individuals are blessed with which gifts. Therefore, it is the Holy Spirit who chooses who will be given the gift of leadership.

However, the selection of leaders does not solely occur through the operation of predestination by a divine being. In 1 Corinthians 12:31a, Paul gives believers the encouragement to look for and desire spiritual talents. Paul has to understand that asking for and seeking a gift might result in one's actually receiving that gift. People who want and try to find the gift of leadership have a chance of accomplishing their goal. People throughout the Bible acquire education and preparation for service, concurrently with the bestowal of spiritual talents in accordance with the free will of God.

The concept and instruction of leadership that his readers receive is influenced by the teachings of the Apostle Paul. In Romans chapter 12, verse 8, the Apostle Paul singles out the gift of leadership as a particular example. On the one hand, it appears that Paul understands leadership to be a distinct and one-of-a-kind spiritual talent, and on the other, he encourages

Christians to make use of the gifts they have been given (Rom. 12:6-8). Paul provides a list of his own gifts and writes about them as though they were predetermined by some fundamental quality (1 Timothy 2:7).

On the other hand, Paul exhorts Timothy to cultivate, train, and educate himself in the application of spiritual gifts (2 Timothy 1:6-7). Paul, like Jesus, served as a guide and counsellor to future leaders. Titus and Timothy are both used here as examples. Paul entrusted these younger men with both responsibility and authority, and then he stepped aside to allow them to lead new congregations. Paul's teaching, while primarily centred on God's sovereign determination of gifts, admits the possibility of human participation in God's gracious choosing. This is despite the fact that Paul's teaching primarily focuses on God's determination of gifts. As a result, engaging in activities aimed at fostering leadership is necessary and proper. Jesus did, in fact, instruct and cultivate future leaders. Paul, an apostle, exhorts individuals to grow in their capacities, and he, like Jesus, made attempts to assist others in developing their ministry skills. Paul encourages people to improve their abilities.

- The Leader Who Is Able To Communicate

Effective communication is one of the most distinguishing characteristics of a leader, setting them apart from other members of the team in a significant way. People are more likely to pay attention to someone who has a command of the English language, and they want the speaker's words to be unambiguous and succinct.

The communicative leader has the capacity to explain the goal in a way that will cause everyone to nod their head in agreement with what they are trying to accomplish. Because of one's capacity to effectively handle communication among the members, problems that arise inside the group can be solved quickly and simply. On the other side, if the leader is unable to connect the dots between the mission and the team, then a plethora of difficulties are almost certain to arise.

Because of his or her capacity to effectively instruct team members, a leader who is good at communicating has the ability to transform an unproductive working atmosphere into one that fosters productivity. This leader also makes it a point to be available for consultation and to be able to listen intently to the thoughts and comments of those around them. At the end of the day, effective communication requires participation from both parties.

The Process of Becoming One:

If you want to be an effective communicative leader, you have to be able to regularly implement the following methods in order to have positive interactions with your team:

Deal with it on a more intimate basis. In front of the team, you should try to avoid giving a lecture and instead focus on making the discussion more engaging. Always use a person's name when addressing them, and make sure to offer questions with open-ended answers so that individuals have the chance to react.

Don't get vague! Avoid using ambiguous language wherever possible, but especially when providing directions and constructive feedback. If you want to avoid confounding other people, remember to be brief, clear, and courteous.

Foster a sense of compassion. The trap of hubris is one that many leaders fall into, and as a result, they wind up believing that they are better than their contemporaries. However, the leader of the team is not the focal point of the group; he or she only fulfils a function within it. You, as the leader, are responsible for displaying empathy towards the other members of the team by trying to put yourself in their shoes and imagining how you would react to the circumstances. You can be of greater assistance to them in finding solutions to their challenges if you demonstrate empathy.

A communicative leader is someone who is able to select the strategy that will work most effectively in any given circumstance. It is important to keep in mind that communication is also cultural; just because humour was successful with one individual does not indicate that it would be successful with another. It is important to be aware of the communication style of the other person and to adapt accordingly.

Be Aware Of What Is Happening In Your Environment.

The last thing that a good leader should bear in mind is how essential it is to have a deep comprehension of the culture that they are a part of. You need to have an understanding of the kinds of products that the people around you want, as well as the reasons why a particular product or service succeeds in a particular culture but fails to succeed in others.

People's means of making decisions, the way they speak and communicate with one another, the tales they tell their children and grandchildren, the myths and legends that are passed down, and the methods of doing work are all fundamental components of culture. It is also about the customs and traditions of a certain location or nation; but, in this case, we are speaking about the culture of your place of employment.

It is also believed that culture is something that can be learnt and that it reveals a great deal about the manner in which the people who live in a particular location behave. What really matters is that you educate yourself on the culture of the location you are in so that you are aware of what you can contribute and so that you can learn more about the people who are in your immediate environment.

How exactly are you supposed to comprehend, or at the very least obtain a feel for, what is occurring in the workplace? You can easily accomplish the following by doing so:

Take Stock of Your Circumstances

Do a quick scan of your environment. You are able to accomplish this goal by asking specific sorts of questions, such as those that will assist you in gaining a better understanding of the situation at hand and in determining what actions you might take next. The following are some examples of possible questions:

Where exactly are all of the many departments that make up your office located?

What kinds of things do people keep on their workstations?

What are some common topics of conversation during breaks?

What do people talk about in their e-mails and letters to one another?

How frequently do individuals use their phones, other electronic devices, and computers?

How would you characterise the tenor of your messages? How do you communicate with other people? Do you present a nice demeanour or do you intimidate them?

What kinds of films and television shows do they enjoy watching? Which songs are now enjoying a lot of success?

What sorts of garments do they put on their bodies?

What can you notice hanging on the walls or posted on the bulletin boards?

What kinds of foods do individuals enjoy eating?

What kinds of things do individuals do in the various regions of your office?

What kind of reactions do people have towards you and towards one another?

What exactly are the contents of your memos?

In addition to that, remember to be observant!

Take a look at the activities going on in the area around you. Check out what others have displayed on their workstations or walls, observe what they are wearing, and make an effort to learn what it is that they enjoy to listen to or watch in their spare time. In this manner, it will be simple for you to comprehend what might be successful and what may not, and it will be simple for you to devise goods and services that will be beneficial to the individuals concerned.

Learn to see past your feelings. Because a person's core beliefs can be inferred from the feelings he experiences, it is essential to have an understanding of the circumstances that either bring them joy or cause them sorrow. You also need to figure out what kinds of things excite them and what kinds of things they could care less about.

Observe the manner in which your followers communicate with one another. You will gain an understanding of what drives them or what causes them to become agitated in this manner. As you can see, the people around you are pretty much a symbol of the individuals you would like to follow you or patronise your products, and as a result, it is absolutely crucial that you know what it is that they want and what they do not want.

Look for hints that aren't being said. You read in a previous chapter about the significance of non-verbal communication; you should work on improving this skill. You should educate yourself not only in the art of nonverbal communication for yourself, but also in the art of interpreting the nonverbal communication of those who are in your immediate environment.

If you keep these things in mind, there is a good chance that you will become the kind of leader that not only you, but also the people around you, will be proud of.

Skills Necessary in Social Interactions

Being a good manager, managing the office, and the management abilities that are required for this activity are not the only aspects of leadership that are important. In order to be an effective leader, you need to have management abilities, but you also need social skills. This is due to the fact that the leader is a social being who invests a significant amount of time connecting with people from all aspects of society. As a manager, he is seen on the shop floor interacting with the machinists; as the chair of the company, she is seen in the boardroom with senior management personnel; as a social activist, she is seen in public spaces advocating for a social cause; as a politician, he is seen in meetings with other political leaders forging a bill; and as a magistrate, she is seen in the courtroom pronouncing judgements that have profound effects on the lives of litigants.

At each and every one of these events, the leader is expected to display his social abilities, which are also sometimes referred to as social graces. It is possible to describe social skills as the art of successfully navigating oneself within social groups. To give just a few examples, the manner in which an individual speaks, eats, gestures, dresses, and walks is one example of such a skill.

The setting of the social event, the goal of the event, and the individuals that make up the social group all have an impact on a person's level of social competence. Because of this, the social skills required for a get-together with friends will be different than those required for an office party.

The social behaviour of followers is frequently determined by how a leader acts in society; in most circumstances, the leader is the role model for society. People in the field of fashion and movies are the ones that set the trend with their attire, and then these designs are made available in stores for the followers to purchase. This is the reason that fashion magazines and movie magazines have such a large fan following. Mahatma Gandhi is an additional illustration of the role of the leader in forming the preferences and sentiments of a society. Gandhi's demonstration of the art of non-violence as a method for resolving conflicts was adopted by Martin Luther King, Jr., during the civil rights movement in the United States, and then again by Nelson Mandela, during the process of dismantling apartheid in South Africa. Both of these men were leaders in their respective movements.

Therefore, in this part of the discussion, we will have a look at a few of the social abilities that define the personality of a leader and set him or her in the forefront of a social grouping.

The Struggles In Private

The journey of every great leader begins within themselves. They never reach to the point where they can lead others without first taking charge of their own life and overcoming the challenges that they face. They are aware of their limitations and draw on those to make themselves stronger. The vast majority of leaders have encountered challenges and grown as a result, becoming significantly more capable than they were in the past.

First and foremost, a Servility Attitude

The best leaders are also excellent followers. They prioritise the needs of others over their own. The people are the priority of real leaders. They put the needs of others ahead of their own and do not think about what they want. They have a fundamental belief that success does not come from the efforts of a single individual, but rather from the collaboration of a group. A good leader would never fail to acknowledge the contributions of the team members who worked on a successful project. Additionally, he or she is quite skilled at following directions. When a leader listens, they listen attentively and try to put themselves in the position of the individuals they are listening to.

When it comes to following directions, good leaders are meticulous and pay attention to the smallest of details. There are some people who have tried to be great leaders but have failed because they are unable to obey even the most basic instructions. The act of following is straightforward, yet not everyone is able to do it simply because they are unable to humble themselves. Simply showing that you are following is a demonstration that you are not higher than everyone else in the room. If you possess this quality, then you have one of the most important attributes of a strong leader: the ability to inspire others.

Self-discipline is the second desirable quality.

Not only does self-discipline require restraint, but it also necessitates the ability to exercise one's own self-control and the bravery to turn down opportunities that involve matters of lesser significance. If you want to be a great leader, you need to first be able to win the internal conflicts that take place within yourself before you can win the battles that take place in the public arena. You can't demand things of other people if you won't even do what you say you're going to do for yourself. When you become a leader, having self-discipline can take you a long way; for this reason, it is essential that you give attention to developing it. The way that you carry yourself and the actions that you take can have an effect on the behaviour of other people.

3. Drive or Enthusiasm

Everyone needs to have a burning desire. They are able to accomplish anything, even if it seems impossible, because of the desire they have. The actions of great leaders are seldom taken simply for the sake of taking action. They spend their time pursuing their passions. They almost always have a group of people on their squad who have the same level of enthusiasm as them. They are never at a loss for anything to strive for or an objective to accomplish.

A good leader always has something that they aim to accomplish in the future. His enthusiasm extends well beyond the duties he must perform and the responsibilities he must fulfil. It is the primary impetus behind everything he does and the energy that propels him forward.

Commitment, the fourth and final quality

It is imperative that you set a good example for your team if you want them to put in their best effort and generate great work. You need to be the example that they follow. There is nothing that can motivate an employee more than seeing the boss putting in the same amount of effort as the rest of the staff. It is always encouraging to see your supervisor putting in effort to get the job done, rather than simply barking orders at everyone else, as this demonstrates a greater level of commitment. You will not only earn the respect of your team but also instill the same devotion and enthusiasm in your employees if you demonstrate how committed you are to achieving the objective of your team and your job as a leader by exhibiting how committed you are to doing so.

In addition to putting in a lot of effort, the best demonstration of commitment is not only finishing the work at hand but also keeping the commitments you make to others. You should fulfil your word whether you offered to throw a party on a Friday night or promised to pay an additional sum of money to your employees as a bonus. You don't just want to earn a name for yourself as a leader who puts in a lot of effort; you also want to be known for being fair. Once you have earned the respect of the entire team, it is more likely that they will offer the level of quality work that you have requested from them.

Responsibility-taking is the focus of the fifth quality.

A good leader is someone who accepts responsibility for their own acts and does not place blame on others for their own mistakes. If you aspire to be a successful leader, you need to be able to develop the skill of learning how to accept responsibility for your actions. If you were unsuccessful in hitting the target, rather than blaming others, look yourself to determine where you went wrong. Instead of berating the entire team for the failed project, you should reflect on what went wrong and take the necessary steps to improve. You are mistaken if you believe that you have the right to wash your hands when things do not go according to the plans that you had made. You have the power to lead your people to success, but you also have the potential to lead them to failure if you so choose.

THE LEADERSHIP, AS WELL AS THE AUTHORITY

Jesse was a young man eager to serve the Lord with all his heart. He had a strong sense that God was calling him to preach, and he had visions of how God would use him to transform the world via his words. However, his pastor never gave him the opportunity to preach during the Sunday service and instead only let him preach to the younger members of the congregation. Jesse, who felt that he had been treated disrespectfully by his pastor, started accepting a lot of invitations to speak in other places. It seems as though God chose to bless him and use his skills largely in settings other than his church.

After a period of time, he parted ways with the church and launched his own ministry, taking with him a number of the congregation's members. After some time, he established his own church. The newly planted church had abundant growth for a number of years. People in the community acknowledged Jesse's status as a preacher and a man of God. However, as time went on, a few of the younger children and teenagers in the church stopped respecting his leadership and started going their own separate ways. His irritation led him to make an effort to persuade them to deepen their commitment to the church. The issue, on the other hand, continued to worsen, and he soon realised that more than half of the youth had stopped attending the church as a result.

Where did we go wrong? In the sphere of authority, Jesse was merely reaping the consequences of his own actions. In common with many other leaders, he lacked a solid comprehension of the spiritual nature of leadership and its implications. We tend to have a negative attitude towards those in power, whether it is in the business sector or the church. We want to be released from the grip that it has over us. We prefer to hold positions of authority rather than be subject to it.

In this chapter, I will examine the biblical concept of authority, focusing in particular on how it pertains to leadership. I will also look at some of the implications of this perspective. The teachings of the Apostle Paul, who was one of the most influential figures in human history, will be the primary subject of this article.

In 1 Corinthians 11:1, Paul instructs the believers, "Follow my example, as I follow the example Christ has set for me." This one verse conveys one of the most important and foundational Christian leadership and authority principles: that true leadership begins with obedience to those in authority over us. Paul encourages the congregation, "Follow me, as I follow." It was only because he himself was following someone else that he was able to convince others to follow him. Only those who are willing to follow are deserving to take the reins of leadership, which is an amusing but true statement. Ben Franklin is credited with coining the phrase "He who cannot obey cannot command."19 If you do not submit to those in charge, you cannot effectively exercise that authority over others.

This is a peculiar way of thinking. Because I was able to convince other people to do what I said, I believed that this made me a leader. But Paul was able to become a leader because, first and foremost, he was a follower. He exhorted the Corinthians, without any sense of embarrassment, to follow him as he followed Christ. Because he was a guy who was subject to authority, he was able to talk with authority. Paul acknowledged both the power that God held over him and the authority that the church held over him. (Two examples of Paul's subjection to the churches in Antioch and Jerusalem may be seen in Acts 14:26–15:4, which can be found here.)

All too frequently, we have a negative perception of those in positions of authority, viewing them as people who place limitations on us and dictate our actions. However, in order for us to make effective use of our positions of power, we need to have a solid comprehension of what authority is and how it works. The Bible outlines four primary elements of power, each of which a leader ought to have a firm grasp on.

Leadership Is A Way Of Behaving Rather Than A Title Or Position.

This indicates that your actions will determine the kind of leader you will be in the future. The fact that you have been promoted does not automatically make you the most effective leader. People have been promoted simply because they have been in the same position for a long time, despite the fact that some of these individuals had the leadership abilities of a wet paper bag. I have seen this happen. You may rest easy knowing that folks who do things like this are eventually exposed. It is possible for anyone, regardless of their status or position, to take on the role of a leader. After completing their training, the majority of officers in the British army are assigned to a specific regiment. There are Soldiers, Corporals, Sergeants, and so on throughout these units that have greater experience than the Officer. The command is depending on these soldiers to take charge until the Officer has a better grasp on the situation. The same thing might happen at a firm when an individual graduates from college and immediately begins working in a managerial capacity. Always remember to act and behave as a leader should, regardless of what position you hold, because your role as a leader requires you to encourage and motivate the people working under your supervision.

The second most effective strategy for swaying other people's opinions is to lead by example.

To summarise, you should never ask another person to carry out an activity that you are unwilling to carry out yourself. For instance, if you wanted everyone to help clean up, you should first delegate responsibilities to the other people, and then get started cleaning up after yourself. It is important to overcome your fear of getting your hands filthy. If you want to be a successful leader, you need to have the guts to take the initiative and do things the right way first. People will see whether you set a good or terrible example and act accordingly, thus it is important to keep in mind that you should always be aware of your surroundings and act accordingly.

Action: Ask everyone to clean up, and then start cleaning up yourself along with your colleagues when everyone else has finished. This approach is also applicable to a variety of other tasks.

The third most important aspect of leadership is having an influence.

Taking this into consideration, it ought to have a positive influence. Someone showing up at their place of employment with the intention of challenging their authority is something I've witnessed far too frequently, and it has a detrimental impact on the atmosphere there. They did have an effect, but it was a negative one on the world.

I had a boss once who, as soon as he took leadership of a new location, sat everyone down, let us take a beer, removed his rank slide, and then proceeded to have a debate lasting between two and three hours regarding the positive and negative aspects of the location. Because of this, he was able to get all of the responses he required from his staff members, as well as a great deal of respect from everyone involved in the process.

Action: Try this out in your place of employment, gather everyone together, and hold an open forum discussion about the positive aspects and negative aspects of your workplace that need to be improved. There should be no ramifications for anything that is stated during these sessions.

Understanding Leadership is the Topic of Leadership 101.

The first thing we need to do is get a better grasp on what leadership actually entails before we can move on to discussing actionable methods and pointers that can help you become a great leader who is also able to influence the behaviour of those around you. The approaches and pointers that were presented will make more sense after you have a firm grasp on the concept of true leadership.

The concept of leadership is one that is widely misunderstood. In point of fact, the vast majority of people believe that leadership is all about superiority and dominance. While it is true that leadership can be achieved via the use of force, this style of leadership is neither sustainable, ethical, or acceptable. In this book, we will be talking about how to build the attributes of a leader that others will respect and naturally WANT to follow. This is the topic that will be covered.

You should make learning a lifelong endeavour and read as much as you can on any topic that interests you, including the issue of leadership. There are many wonderful gurus out there who can go into great detail about all of the ways in which you can be a great leader. I encourage you to make learning a lifelong endeavour and read as much as you can on any topic that interests you. However, in this article, we are going to provide you with a condensed version of the information necessary to become an excellent leader. Do not be misled by the brevity of this book; the information contained within these pages has the potential to transform your status within any group dynamic into that of a leader, provided that you use it in a consistent manner.

Who Are the People Who Lead?

As opposed to what is commonly believed, being a leader involves a great deal more than simply holding the highest position in an organisation or being the one who issues directives to others. It is possible to hold a position of authority while simultaneously lacking the self-assurance, experience, and personality traits necessary to motivate people to willingly cooperate with one another towards the accomplishment of a shared objective in order to reach a successful conclusion.

Who, then, has the role of a leader? Someone who keeps their word is the definition of a leader. A capable leader is one who is also fair and has an open mind. A real leader would never ask followers to do something that they themselves wouldn't be willing to do. A leader is someone who recognises when something needs to be done and then does it on their own without being asked. A good leader is one who is always willing to learn and to teach others. A good leader is compassionate and inspiring to others around them. A good leader fights alongside his team, accepts responsibility for the losses that the team suffers, and provides credit to his team for any successes that they achieve. A leader is someone whose words, actions, and body language have a positive influence on others to the point where they feel driven to put in their best effort to keep things going. This compels them to follow the leader's example and provide their best efforts to the success of the endeavour.

If you work towards attaining the attributes described above, other people will naturally WANT to follow your lead. When you employ coercion as a form of leadership, your followers will not respect you, productivity will be at an all-time low, and the dynamic of the workplace will be unpleasant. This is not leadership; rather, it is acting in a supervisory capacity. Continue reading this article if you want to build a long-lasting leadership position that is founded on the respect and believe of others in you.

Don't worry about the fact that the characteristics of character needed to be an effective leader may seem like a heavy order to fulfil; with enough experience, all of those qualities will become second nature. It is NEVER too late to begin developing into the person you have ALWAYS DREAMED of being. What we present to the outside world is an image of ourselves that we've concocted based on our surroundings, our upbringing, our education, our self-image, the values that we hold, and the beliefs that we have. Once you are conscious of this fact, you will be able to initiate the process of developing new convictions and principles, as well as altering the kind of personality you have.

Now that you have a better grasp of what it takes to be a leader, we will delve a little deeper into how to develop and put these abilities and attributes into practise so that you can become a better leader.

Learn Your Own Method Of Leadership.

The first step in becoming an effective leader is figuring out what kind of leader one already is. There are essentially four distinct kinds of leaders, and they are all on an even playing field. The only thing that differentiates them is how they carry out their leadership and how well they can connect with other people. These categories are as follows:

Leaders with the Courage to Lead. Even when confronted with a difficult situation, people like this never lose sight of their long-term objectives and vision. They are aware of their goals, and they understand how to uphold the principles that guide them. In this day and age, it is necessary to learn how to be true to yourself and how to stick to your gut because it is basically what you will have left, amidst all the changes. It is important to learn how to be true to yourself and how to stick to your gut because it is basically what you will have left. People will come to the conclusion that you are someone who is worthy of being emulated if you are able to maintain your authenticity.

Leaders Who Are Servants. If you have a high level of concern for the people you supervise, you are most likely the servant-type of leader. They frequently inquire about how they may be of assistance to others and frequently consider ways in which things might be improved upon and altered. They don't just sit in the office and delegate all of their responsibilities to others; rather, they get their hands dirty with whatever it is that they're responsible for. In addition to thinking, they get their hands dirty. They are also kind and charitable, and they are willing to assist people in any manner that they can.

Leaders who can inspire others. Inspirational leaders are leaders who are committed to their beliefs and values and who can motivate others to do the same. They inspire others to believe that change is possible and that if they put their minds and souls into anything, they will be able to achieve whatever goal they set for themselves. They frequently exhibit new thinking and a focus on the future. They don't believe in limitations and think the possibilities are essentially limitless because of this. They don't conform to the here and now; instead, they focus on the future and what they can do to influence it.

Influential Thinkers. Leaders of thought make use of their minds and have the mindset that they can always improve their knowledge as long as they continue to live. They open people's eyes to the fact that education does not end in the classroom and that there is a great deal more about the world that each and every person should be aware of. They earn the increased respect of those who follow them by demonstrating to them that change is possible and that they have the potential to do great things for themselves and the world. People adore them because of the change they are able to bring about in the world.

So, tell me about the kind of leader you are.

Keep in mind that it is essential to determine the kind of leader you are so that you can have more conviction as a person and, as a result, have greater influence over those who report to you. If you have a strong sense of self-identity, it will be difficult for others to tear you down, and it will be simple for you to serve as an example to others. If you are aware of who you are, you will have a far better chance of doing the things you set out to do.

One Type of Treatable Anxiety Disorder Is Social Anxiety

Anxiety caused by a constant dread of being watched and evaluated by other people is the defining feature of the mental illness known as social anxiety.

This may sound incomprehensible to someone who has never struggled with social anxiety or been afraid of the people in their immediate environment. Why would you be afraid of other people? Could it be fear, and if so, is it possible to overcome it? What is so terrible that you reach a point where experiencing panic attacks is unavoidable, and it doesn't go better no matter what you do?

It is easy to misunderstand social anxiety. It can be incredibly constraining and feel plain dreadful to be in a situation in which the last thing you want to do is enter a room full of people. If you have nightmares in which you know you have to deliver a speech the next day or be faced with a crowd in any form, this can make the situation even worse. It's not like folks who struggle with social anxiety made a conscious decision to acquire this characteristic. Are you able to get past it? Probably not, but with a lot of effort and training, you can learn how to tolerate it better and have a better experience overall. Because social anxiety is so poorly understood, people have a tendency to pass judgment on those who suffer from it. People who suffer from social anxiety are often misunderstood and categorized as shy or even introverted rather than receiving the help they need to understand their condition. It's very similar like climbing a ladder. You are first regarded as being reserved, then as being introverted, and finally, all of a sudden, you are thought of as being "weird" or unusual.

Now, being unique isn't necessarily a negative thing because no one in the annals of achievement has ever asserted that it's necessary to be precisely the same as the folks standing next to you in order to achieve success. Nevertheless, if it restricts you in any way, that kind of difference isn't all that impressive. Even if people tell you it's not, social anxiety disorder is a different case, and believe me when I say that it's a wonderful thing to be different.

People who suffer from social anxiety disorder typically deny that they have a mental illness. The vast majority of the time, they don't even give it a second thought. They are, as we have stated previously, reserved, introverted, peculiar, and could possibly be categorized as socially uncomfortable. Nobody appreciates having it, and the majority of people wish they could get rid of it, particularly when it prevents you from doing typical things as other people do them. This includes having an easy time meeting new people or conversing with strangers, dating, freely expressing oneself in public, making eye contact with others, going to parties and other social events, dining in front of other people, routinely attending school or work, and seeking out conversions. People who suffer from social anxiety may have one of these limitations, or all of them, which is caused by the belief that they are being judged by other people, the fear of drawing attention to themselves or upsetting another person, or the feeling of being ashamed or humiliated. A traumatic event in the past, such as being bullied or having low self-esteem, can also be a contributing factor in experiencing social anxiety.

Everyone's experience of social anxiety is unique to them, as is their reaction to pressure and stress. It is vital to address it in whatever way you are able to given that it stops you from living a healthy life and possibly creating healthy connections, and given that doing so is necessary.

Even though it could appear to be impossible to conquer, there is a technique to deal with social anxiety, even though it might be hard to believe at first. It is especially true given that persons who experience it have a need to form friendships, become active in social activities, and participate in groups. If this is the case, then why do people display such a significant amount of restraint? Why do people feel unable to interact with others or speak when they are in a social context because of this fear? However, participation is not optional. It is impossible to change the situation. In spite of the fact that these people harbor anxieties and fears over the situation, the only way for them to effect change is to confront them. Interacting with other people who are experiencing the same issue is the only way to find a solution to it. Even though they are afraid of it, people who suffer from social anxiety have a strong desire to interact with the people around them in a social, pleasant, and open manner. However, they are unable to do so because of their anxiety. One solution could be to join a support group with other individuals who struggle with the same issue.

In addition to physical symptoms, those who suffer from social anxiety sometimes experience emotional triggers. These include feelings of anxiousness, negative emotional cycles, blushing, a racing heartbeat, dry mouth and throat, excessive sweating, and muscle twitching. When it is activated, you may have severe anxiety, and you may even develop a bodily dysmorphia and become highly self-conscious. In this state, you may view yourself in an unfavorable or unreasonable light, which may lead to distorted perceptions of the world around you. People who suffer from social anxiety are typically aware of how unreasonable their condition is; nonetheless, their feelings and anxieties continue to be persistent and continue to be chronic. The majority of the time, you may get the impression that it doesn't make a difference what you do; it just won't go away. It was said previously that cognitive behavioral therapy, also known as CBT, is believed to be an effective remedy for it since it modifies the way the neural pathways work in the brain, which brings hope to those who are suffering from the repercussions of their everyday restraints and feelings.

The first step toward recovery is to get help and have your disease diagnosed by an expert who is familiar with the appropriate treatment for your condition. Active behavioral therapy is an essential component of cognitive behavioral therapy (CBT) and helps patients work through their problem while also working through real-life challenges with other members of their group during group sessions. You will, in time, acquire the skills necessary to approach and easily manage the obstacles that social anxiety brings to the table for you. With the appropriate treatment, support, patience, and effort, it can be transformed into a condition that can be treated. Changing your ideas, feelings, and behavior in response to other people and social situations can be accomplished with the help of cognitive behavioral therapy (CBT). You will have success in recovering from your disorder if you are compliant with the necessary steps to conquer it and if you do what is required of you.

www.ingramcontent.com/pod-product-compliance
Lightning Source LLC
Chambersburg PA
CBHW052145110526
44591CB00012B/1871